TWINS MAC & MADI GO CAMPING

By Linda Herron

Illustrated By Marie Delon

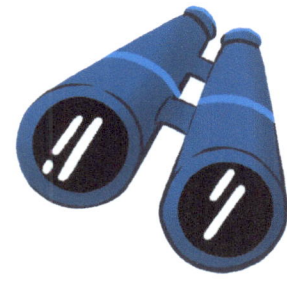

Twins Mac & Madi Go Camping

This is a work of fiction. Names, characters, places, and incidents either are the product of the author's imagination or are used fictitiously. Any resemblance to actual persons, living or dead, events, or locales is entirely coincidental.

Copyright © 2023 by Linda Herron

All rights reserved. No part of this book may be reproduced or used in any manner without written permission of the copyright owner except for the use of quotations in a book review. For more information, email address: Linda@BigLittlePress.com

First edition July 2023
Book design by Project 100
Book cover design by Michelle Gruyé-Hallam

ISBN9781959140092 (hardcover)

www.BigLittlePress.com

Publisher's Cataloging-In-Publication Data
(Prepared by the Cassidy Cataloguing Services)

Names: Herron, Linda, author. | Delon, Marie, illustrator.

Title: Twins Mac & Madi Go Camping / Linda Herron ; illustrations by Marie Delon.

Other titles: Twins Mac and Madi Go Camping

Description: First edition. | [San Jose, California] : Big Little Press, [2023] | Series: Twins Mac & Madi ; [book 6] | Interest age level: 003-008. | Summary: Get your tents and prepare for an amazing camping trip with twins Mac and Madi! Whether your idea of fun is canoeing in a crystal-clear lake, hiking with friends through the forest, or singing songs around the campfire while enjoying delicious s'mores, kids and adults alike will adore this cute rhyming story as they discover all the joys of the Great Outdoors.--Publisher.

Identifiers: ISBN: 9781959140085 (paperback) | 9781959140092 (hardcover) | 9781959140078 (ebook)

Subjects: LCSH: Twins--Juvenile fiction. | Sisters--Juvenile fiction. | Camping--Juvenile fiction. | Outdoor recreation--Juvenile fiction. | CYAC: Twins--Fiction. | Sisters--Fiction. | Camping--Fiction. | Outdoor recreation--Fiction. | LCGFT: Stories in rhyme. | Action and adventure fiction.

Classification: LCC: PZ7.1.H49465 Twc 2023 | DDC: [E]--dc23

DEDICATION TO

Writing the dedication page for my book as an indie author was an easy decision. *Twins Mac & Madi Go Camping* was inspired by my summers spent camping with my Grandparents. I could not have authored this book without them. They brought to life the joys and laughter that only camping can bring. Even now, as I hold this book in my hands, those memories come flooding back, and I can't help but smile. So, with great enthusiasm and warmth, I dedicate this book to Mem and Pep who gave me such beautiful and unforgettable moments.

Thank you for inspiring me to write this story!

Linda Herron
xoxo

"Mac!" "Madi!" says Mom and Dad, and the twins open their eyes. "We're going on a camping trip," their parents say. "SURPRISE!"

Mac and Madi jump out of bed, their faces full of glee.
"A camping trip?" They shout with joy. "How lucky can we be?"

They change their clothes. They pack their bags.
They help load up the car.
The travel to the camping site—it isn't very far.

While Mom and Dad set up the camper and unpacked all the gear.
Mac and Madi explored the lake without an ounce of fear.

They meet a bunch of other kids, and soon they are all friends. Then all the families go on a hike until the nature trail ends.

They have some lunch. They play some games.
They cool off in the lake.
Then all the children shriek and jump
when they see a tiny snake.

The sun starts to set, their tummies rumble,
and Dad lights up the grill.
Mac and Madi eat burgers and hot dogs
until they've had their fill.

Mom starts the campfire, they gather 'round.
They tell stories and sing.
Then they settle inside their cozy camper.
What will tomorrow bring?

When morning comes, Mom asks the twins,
"What do you want to do?"
Madi says, "I want to fish!" But Mac says, "No, canoe!"

"Don't worry—we have lots of time," Mom tells the twins.
"We'll go fishing first, and then canoe,
and that way, everyone wins!"

"That settles it!" says Dad, and he jumps up with a grin.
"Let's set up our fishing poles and see what we reel in!"

"I'm going to catch the very first fish!" says Madi with a shout.
"No, *I* am!" says Mac. "A really giant trout!"

But Dad catches the first fish—then Madi, then Mom, then Mac.
They take some pictures and then throw the fish back.

"Dad may have caught the first fish", says Mac.
"But I had the most fun."
"No, I did!" Madi exclaims. "So, we both are number one!"

Next, they put on life vests and climb into a canoe.
They argue over where they'll sit
(because that's just what twins do).

Then they begin to paddle, and the twins have so much fun.
Neither Mac nor Madi are ready for it to be done.

When nighttime falls, they start a fire
and invite all their new friends.
They sing, tell jokes, and laugh with glee,
and hope the night never ends.

The twins tell everyone a story about a not so scary ghost,
Then Mom says, "Gather 'round the fire—
we have marshmallows to roast!"

They roast their marshmallows, make their s'mores,
and end up with sticky fingers,
It's past their bedtime, but no one cares—
everyone sits and lingers.

They look up at the sparkling sky and point out the moon and stars.
They catch twinkling fireflies and place them inside jars.

When it's finally time to go to bed,
the twins go inside their camper.
With smiles on their faces and the day was free of tempers.

Then Mac and Madi lay side-by-side, and as they fall asleep.
They tell each other secrets that they know they'll always keep.

When morning comes, it's time to leave,
and Mac and Madi are so sad.
But they'll never forget their camping trip
and all the fun they had.

On the ride home, Mom asks, "What part did you like best? There are no right or wrong answers because this is not a test."

"The best part was canoeing," says Mac,
"and swimming in the lake."
"No, the best part was fishing," says Madi,
"except seeing that creepy snake!"

"But what about the s'mores?" asks Mom.
"And all the friends you made?"
"What about the songs we sang,
and all the games we played?"

Then Mac and Madi look out the window
at the sunshiny weather.
They share a glance and say,
"The best part was being together!"

HAPPY CAMPING EVERYONE!

Author Linda Herron

Linda is a children's author, proud Rhode Islander, and identical twin who loves to craft heartwarming tales about the magic bond between siblings. With first-hand experience of the joys and struggles that being an identical twin entails, Linda was inspired to write a series of fun children's stories to help kids embrace their differences and cherish their special relationship with their sister or brother.

As a seasoned financial expert by day, when Linda isn't dreaming up new children's stories to delight and entertain her readers, she's writing business articles and blogs. Her financial expertise has been featured on major media outlets including American Express, LendingTree, and Daily Business News. Currently, Linda enjoys the sunny weather in California, but she often returns to Rhode Island to spend time with her beloved family. For more information about Linda and her books, visit her website at www.lherron.com.

Illustrator Marie Delon

Marie is a Mexican illustrator based in the city of Puebla, Mexico. Her work is characterized by its digital techniques and mixed media, which she employs in her illustrations for independent publications and zines, children's books, and advertising - both national and international. As a full-time graphic designer, Marie also implements her illustrations into her daily job. Recently, she has been working on personal creative projects that include character design, merchandising design, and concept art for videogames. In her spare time, Marie loves watching movies, reading comic books, and playing tabletop RPG games.

www.ingramcontent.com/pod-product-compliance
Lightning Source LLC
LaVergne TN
LVHW072312090526
838202LV00019B/2269